P9-DGE-904

DATE DUE

WITHDRAWN

**SCHAUMBURG TOWNSHIP
DISTRICT LIBRARY
130 SOUTH ROSELLE ROAD
SCHAUMBURG, ILLINOIS 60193**

THE NATIONAL POETRY SERIES

The National Poetry Series was established in 1978 to publish five books of poetry every year through participating trade publishers. Publication of the books is funded by James Michener, Edward J. Piszek, the Copernicus Society, the Witter Bynner Foundation for Poetry, Patricia Robinson, the Mobil Foundation, and the five publishers: Random House, Doubleday & Company, E. P. Dutton, Harper & Row, and Holt, Rinehart and Winston.

THE NATIONAL POETRY SERIES—1983

Donald Revell, *From the Abandoned Cities* (Selected by C. K. Williams)
Joanne Kyger, *Going On: Selected Poems 1958–1980*
          (Selected by Robert Creeley)
Jane Miller, *The Greater Leisures* (Selected by Stanley Plumly)
Susan Tichy, *The Hands in Exile* (Selected by Sandra McPherson)
John Yau, *Corpse and Mirror* (Selected by John Ashbery)

FROM
THE ABANDONED
CITIES

FROM
THE ABANDONED
CITIES

Poems by DONALD REVELL
Winner of the Open Competition
The National Poetry Series

Selected by C. K. WILLIAMS

HARPER & ROW, PUBLISHERS, New York
Cambridge, Philadelphia, San Francisco, London
Mexico City, São Paulo, Sydney

SCHAUMBURG TOWNSHIP PUBLIC LIBRARY
32 WEST LIBRARY LANE
SCHAUMBURG, ILLINOIS 60194

"In Lombardy," "Central Park South," "Odile," "Aesthete's Complaint," and "Mignonette" first appeared in *Antaeus.*

"Near Life" and "Graves in East Tennessee" first appeared in *Black Warrior Review.*

"Gymnopedie: The Exhibition" first appeared in *New England Review.*

"Satiesme," "No Moment," and "A Few Discretions" first appeared in *Poem.*

"Motel View," "Rodeo Aesthetique," "Animaux," and "Theriot Cove" first appeared in *Poetry.*

FROM THE ABANDONED CITIES. Copyright © 1983 by Donald Revell. All rights reserved. Printed in the United States of America. No part of this book may be used or reproduced in any manner whatsoever without written permission except in the case of brief quotations embodied in critical articles and reviews. For information address Harper & Row, Publishers, Inc., 10 East 53rd Street, New York, N.Y. 10022. Published simultaneously in Canada by Fitzhenry & Whiteside Limited, Toronto.

FIRST EDITION

Designer: Sidney Feinberg

Library of Congress Cataloging in Publication Data

Revell, Donald.
    From the abandoned cities.

    (The National poetry series)
    I. Title.   II. Series.
PS3568.E793F7   1983   811'.54   82-48677
ISBN 0-06-015167-6   83 84 85 86 87 10 9 8 7 6 5 4 3 2 1
ISBN 0-06-091058-5 (pbk.)   83 84 85 86 87 10 9 8 7 6 5 4 3 2 1

8/84
MAR-ROW

811
REVELL, D

3 1257 00365 3945

To William Stein

CONTENTS

"If poetry is not absolution"—he whispered to himself—
"then we can expect pity from nowhere else."
Yannis Ritsos

I

TO BEGIN

Some love, and a short stay in a public garden
is the real matter. Pauses, the intervals

that strayed on, becoming a life, limn these, color.
Once, an allure was best and one's was unbroken.

Only now, the ghost drawn in figure, at Christall,
is a broken haunt, and you can't love her.

A ROAD AND CLOUDS

1.
The bright hills followed like talk and the ride was easy.
The dead springs, the Imperial Baths' blue
against orange leaves went dark in the car's long shadow
and then shone. For miles, the towns were a cool light
on the county road. We stopped at a waterfall.
In plashes, the clear stream headed down over rocks
and ended flared in a deep pool among shadows.
"Other lives," she said, "cloud this, leading us on
in grey figures lifted from an old travelogue.
Look there." We left, a last town outrunning the dark
by minutes as the night caught on. The abandoned
houses, the failed sky broken by hills in blue
swirls thinned and were lost. With big times ahead, we talked
as a girl's voice from the car radio kept singing.

2.
"Today, we are the thin youngsters paired in a love
story. The city, a dressed cloud running rings
around parks, is where it happens. Remember *Tristan;*
the streets will smile." In a concourse of intimacies,
other lives dreamed crowds and the buildings narrowed.
Over the first thin trees of the park, birds plunged
in signs. We walked to a gallery. There, couples
drifted among Rothkos or sat in the iron
chairs to look at the statue. After a while,
we left. A retrieved light struck us, its faded amber
contrasting with the grey sky and crowds; it followed
us back. At home, the window darkened like sky

as amber streaks marked paths on the city. "Look
there," she said. The view was all lines and ringed spaces.

3.
Birds started. A slow flare over the lawns at Christall
branched into sky. In clear lines, the trees threw shade.
We held to small dreams or to the vague figures morning
limned as we woke. The house got lively. A restrained
warmth, a chime, rose from the sunny terrace and we
went down. Rooms flashed along the hall in a calm
progress. "You would expect," she said, "that the place
would sing at the eaves or burn down, but look—only
the light is broken." The sunlight branched from the terrace
and there was coffee and a good view of the lawns
outside. All morning, chinaberries performed
slow figures in the heavy air. Above
them, birds flew in galleries. The scenic clutter,
the retrieved signs followed like marked paths, then faded.

IN LOMBARDY

She mocks the bones in you, as if it had
been Lombardy you met in, and around
the time of Da Vinci, the man who painted her,
an unboxed body at the center of a sad
procession, womanly, in the veil of a drowned
innocent, and in control. The myrrh,
the acolytes attending, these conjoin
with the figure into an adequate conceit
for what is meant by fear of dying. Her
relationship to the thing is not the point
however, nor is that humiliating street

through which she is attended by the boys
the course of it. Germane to all who swing
the censer, chant, or carry candles are
those inamoratas, those comic angels poised
as if in mockery or blackface, wing
to wing in jibing constellations, stars
in rows. Perfection, the maestro's real intent
is laughter, alive as its direction toward
the living drowned, the lucky ones. Effect,
a countereffect, and the seduction were all meant
to mock us, to seduce our hearts and record
us, aching in ourselves that way. What was intact

was deformed. There was also that fear's result, and what
love means, considering. It means the blank
regard of one's own feet as they progress
along the assigned paths, recalling those facts,
this dread. It means a failing brain at the brink

of hypnosis, permanently. Being less
and more than that, the woman died to be
an object in the mind's expansion, to appear
expansively, as what we desire: a pale
seductress robed in gauze, a fantasy
in black or red or anything as near
a privacy like Ruth's, when alien. Regale

the visual and be recorded, that
is what the body was to have required
of us. Yet if laughter failed, if what took place
did not amuse the angels nor permit
the minds attending to be so inspired
as to collapse upon themselves, her face
alone might have done it. Having been close
enough, there is, in the death, a single thought
whose mystery can be almost comic. In
that, only those accompanying her or those
particular amours that she had brought
to Lombardy for the occasion, loves

born of another hand's intention, could
take part. The face is beautiful. These men
she mocks, the redundant, particular ones, perform
for her, are the desperately in need and would,
without a doubt, be no impediment
to her complete possession of their more
aesthetic realities, their minds as well
as of their senses. Love, for our
enchanting lady, is an abstracted grove
of familiar symbols where a mind can swell
like music, overcome by its own power
to invent, without compassion and above

regalia. As an event, the woman continues,
is in our eyes, by moments indiscrete
or present, then and now depending on
the mind or eyes of imaging. The tense
deformity, the actual defeat
of time through her specific love, is bond
and compact, then, and more than likely years
from then, as well as now in Lombardy
or there in Leonardo's picture. Made
by thoughts of death into a living fear
of bodies, we define a landscape. She
records us in it, weeping, nearly mad.

THE BLUE, THE DEAD ONE

It is from inside a circle you see flame.
No faith, no way beyond what I see, I stand
dumb, off of center, neither hurt nor saved.

But it was never her blue tongue on mine
or the words she wrote. She never touched me. Now,
when she says "blue" on the telephone, I laugh.

And it was never anyone else's heart
I held. They mostly smiled. The one I'd wanted
was killed nine days ago on a subway. Now *you*

laugh, thinking it is all too much. You're right.
It is from inside a circle you see flame.
The blue, the dead one aren't here. They're gone.

CENTRAL PARK SOUTH

The way the buildings curve (as if a thought
or big dream you could never really get
your brain to go about fixing for you, had
for once become a grand hotel, an all-
forgiving grey exterior like that
which faces north across the park and loves
you) makes you think of any afternoon
at five in late October and of how
the girl you followed used to disappear
into the Plaza. Nothing has changed along
that street. You walk. You watch a limousine
go by and look for actresses. The light
is still what you remember having thought of
when you thought of Venice, Henry James,
or being happy—blue, with a touch of grey
and orange. Only your nerves can rot; the rest
goes on discriminating, particularly
places. There have always been those places,
real corners that can stay there and forgive your
wanting a drink or having once believed
that love should be conducted openly
and in the daytime. If you could wrap your mind
around the park, the way these walls do, you
would rot a little more slowly. Maybe if
you dreamed the way a building dreams you
might even heal. Remembering that girl
was not a bad way to start. Just follow her
along the park side now, but go west, away
from that hotel that always put an end
to everything. At Columbus, turn and head

for the museum where they put the bones
together; you will be glad of bones by then,
or with a bit of luck, be side by side
with the girl, having forgotten. But either way,
romantic Venice is alive in New York
again. The lights are as blue as ever; the park
is colorful at night, in October. What
you came for were the curves. You got them. Look
at how the buildings curve around and close
in lovingly. You had been following love
then. Now it is a street beside the park.

MOTEL VIEW

It is conceivable in fact that waves
and lustre work in such a way, in such
a mannered disproportion, that the sea
becomes an architectural conceit
with which to play upon the measure of
a liquid give and take, a weathering. Wave
and the measurement of it can therefore do
but little to intensify the spume
of water in the sun. Cape Ann today
is seascape, rock, and a freezing wind. The moon
is nearly full, but risen far too soon
to have its proper place in the postcard, sun-
light being quite the thing for photographs,
the elderly, and a decent view of the gulls.
(When thinking back, it is the elderly
that one remembers most, enclosed by gulls
and glaring eastward like the benches.) Wave
and lustre mannered to a fault, the cold
vacationland in April, all combine
into a law of things, an intellect
of various disproportions, which, by day,
can sometimes contradict the weather, give
one's time a fiction, or, as water does,
an elemental dullness, an expanse.

GYMNOPEDIE: THE EXHIBITION

She stood on a small bridge over floating lilies,
waved, then moved to the next canvas just
like that. It was as at Coney Island when
they'd put a face in the hole and take a picture:
a woman with the body of a boy
running from haze to cloud, blue haze to bluer
cloud, getting everyone excited. Some
whole lives are vivid cartoons where bodies, each
one more unlikely than the ones before, leap
through frames. Some people's eyes must burn as mine did.

One night we sat and held hands watching *Death
Takes a Holiday.* At the part where our grim hero
has the emotion, we both laughed. She went
to the window where she yelled his great line down
to Montague Street, still laughing. The next day,
the Monet exhibition opened and we
made plans. It's the way these things match up—death, laughter;
laughter, Giverny—that gets ridiculous
even when I remember they had meanings,
repercussions that changed years to clouds.

Some people's eyes must burn as mine did. Every-
body sees things that shouldn't hurt but do
and then goes home and dreams about them. The way
she went from one painting to another all
that morning, trailing the green of one into
the blue of another with quick twists of her
body hurt me. It made me disbelieve
the future as I entered it for good and all.

SCHAUMBURG TWP. PUBLIC LIBRARY

We left the exhibition hand in hand.
The small bridge between then and now broke there.

I think of how things match up sometimes and see
things burning up with light at Giverny.
Loving the souvenirs gets harder. Women
die. The old movies and the exhibition
posters turn into fads, like plants or Egypt,
lose or maybe trade off that intimate
"connectedness" that makes them special. It's
too late to introduce anything else now.
Memory gets stuck into a few
words that won't jibe, and then it's even later.

NEAR LIFE

The small circle in the field goes brown with wind.
Percussive days now, tail off or bend in a picture
that forgives you nothing. The years spent,
the remarks. It is the wind through tall wires

of weed you've named, and that only, the dry noise
on all this ground, better than a human's, best
for these flats. You've called it yours, took it inside you
for loneliness so that now, in these days, its virtue

of being live to no end could be yours also.
And light too, sometimes your own, a narrow passage
back to the dark house in the diminished
clearing. It is like arriving at home:

beloved, unexpected even in the best dream,
and wholly impossible. Wind. Light. The virtues
of a caught self turned inside out as days
bang, darken, are the elements you have.

And later, hauled to the disappearing end
of the field in dream, you stare as they leave you: flamed
cloud tearing east to the living world you can't
fit. Left behind is better. It is the way

things last. Too far from the house to find your way,
you stand quiet. Dawn feints out past the next field,
but does not come. The dream goes on anyway.
The years you have spent like this are what make you glad.

GRAVES IN EAST TENNESSEE

Of the stones you still can read, a third are children's.
Some, the unnamed ones mostly, share a date
with a woman next to them. Together, these
continue to refuse the world in white letters.

The iron fence is down on three sides. The fourth,
containing the low gateposts, faces the road
and, across that, the trailer that looks down
across the valley where big shadows move

and change. Of all the places they could put
a trailer, why just there between the dead
and the view the dead had taken in exchange
for lives? As always, the transient wins out

over the native because it is always,
having been schooled by dispossession, stronger.
And since the faith of these white stones grew out
of dispossession and its cruel, vague hope,

perhaps it's good that they should face the trailer
and the plaster Mexican with his mule cart
full of flowers. Each can comfort each
with impermanence, with gospel: "This is not

our home." The fencing that still stands, absurd
as its dividing weed from weed, the dead
from the absent is, makes that point clear. The ground
it tries and fails to isolate is no

one's home, just as the ground beneath the trailer
is or will soon be no one's. In a while,
the dead will have their view restored to them.
The plaster Mexican will have moved on.

ALBEMARLE

Light paling into less than light
is all you can see of it for now,
my only, my forgotten country.
The white sky collapsed onto white land

is all you can see of it for now
and that hates, hurt prospects flattening
the white sky collapsed onto white land.
You'd thought of it before as love,

and that hates, hurt prospects flattening
even the blanks desire fills.
You'd thought of it before as love
rose, plaintive, like a kind of memory.

Even the blanks desire fills
took forms, half-lives, as in allegory.
Rose, plaintive, like a kind of memory
flowered in that place then,

took forms, half-lives, as in allegory.
It could have been anything scarred, whole
flowered in that place then,
and you'd have believed in its past and loved.

It could have been anything scarred, whole
light paling into less than light,
and you'd have believed in its past and loved
my only, my forgotten country.

BELFAST

Go north any way and sadness clings to the ground
like fog. The sound of voices goes wrong and can't
be followed. You hear, you breathe cries with a damp wind.

Go north to the ruined counties where girls chant
over a piece of wood called "Doll-Who's-Dead"
and where the streets that you walk are a dead giant

who won't rise. Here, History is the unfed
beast past scaring who comes down from the hills
in daylight. It kills anything, in broad

daylight, then is itself stalked until
the men corner it in some back street. They save
the town for the next beast the granite hills

won't hold. And here, Journey's End is the grey
wall, bled white in patches, that divides
bare yard from bare yard, the unsaved from the unsaved.

In the forlorn business of taking sides,
the rain and the rituals of grief have no
part. Each renews the other as each abides

into the next day's routine, into the slow
recessionals of grief and steady rain.
Here, one death's as just as its counterpart as both

right nothing and are only as wrong as the changes
they were meant but failed to bring about.
Here, suffering betrays itself in exchange

for a dead march, too wise to ever doubt
that life has no grander end than a parade
into the next street. The bold dead are borne out

of trouble, brought closer to the sea and laid
down. The living are marched back by pipes to their
reprisals in the bare yards. From either side

of walls that bleed, voices you can't trace rise and tear
the wind into mad gusts. Tomorrow, History
returns. Tonight, the ruined counties prepare.

II

ODILE

Later that night, I thought of her, and of
the bells she wore. A swan in death, she fell
into the music I had wanted love
to be, and ended there. I cannot tell
you much of her beyond that dying. It
was absolute. My lamp had been a bare
intelligence until she died, a fit
of pointless energy at which to stare
and be annihilated like a bug
in summer. Death refashioned light with her
collapse, and made the corpse upon my rug
a thing to love. The swan became a blur
in bed, and I lay quiet, thinking. Birds
flew rings around a house too round for words.

JUST LORD

You are that color in the air I love
and myself, and might have saved me. Have I held
on pointlessly, forgetting that hard days live
in you and are returned through nightmare? Hell
is that one dream I cannot give up to you.
If, holding on, I fell, it was my sick
heart kept me living and hating the world's use
of the afflicted for mere color. More pricks
than kicks is their framed adage, and as I read
it now, it has kept credence. There is neither
hope nor love in anyone, is there? Need
is the one good you allow, the one grace, whether
or not we twist it into the wrong love
of you. I need you and am yours to make live.

RODEO AESTHETIQUE

A generative loathing overcame
them all in turn: the great, I mean, the mad
and nearly so, who by their words became
the kind of filth we most admire; who had,
instead of feeling, speech, instead of time,
the lack of it with which to plot a scene
and make it go. Astride a pantomime
chimera, man and artist act or mean
to act in such a way as to confuse
the public mind's conception of the beautiful
with decorative nothings, blanks abused
by meaning, until with practice, they, the dutiful
enormities, belie their fiction, fall,
and greet chimeras, gazing up, appalled.

BAL DES ARDENTS

1.
Our deaths, the fires we invite by need,
fit effect to rage. We burn and so are freed

of the anger life becomes after infancy,
of the absurd challenges days deal. That we

are wasted to no end is the light we give
you, for virtue. It completes us. It may survive

us, feed the flames a while longer. The wild act
upheld beyond itself by an effect.

We burn. We run to the screams and back, to white
arms lifted in despair and back. Tonight

concludes an argument we've had with our lives.
In waste, we find the excess excess forgives.

2.
Of what am I but these others? Their
brief violence gives a name to what
I could not name, their obscenity
a rude cause to hopelessness. If what
I am is one of these, dancing, I
am assumed into Death's chivalry.

The others have their hysteria.
Unmoved in the fire, I see as light
sees, through the forms that fail, to that

one emptiness each returns to. White
Hart. Fleur-de-Lys. These others whose cries
are answered by scorn in histories.

3.
It was too horrible to be made up or
embellished. I remember holding out
my arms and stepping back. I called the name
of each that burned as he burned, took one step back
for each. The future ended then, as burnt
leaves rising upon thermals from a fire

end: withered, blackened, insubstantial. What
remained was the sick joke we have for life.
Some nights now I stretch out my arms to nothing,
call the names, and wake into a fear
too absolute to name or to live with. They
died first and horribly. I follow, close.

4.
There is the heat that continues, the bad light.
What an event comes down to is less than these,
as here, now, I can neither hear the screams
shrill, shot through flames, nor mourn anyone. The White

Harts, Fleurs-de-Lys. What emblems can I love
or lose or awaken to the dumb regret
of here, where only I am and fear has names?
I read the chronicles that scorn the obscene,

mad boys. Unlike them, like you, I am past wasting.
Excess punishes me, never forgives.
Our deaths, the fires we will fight and lose
to, arrive coolly and last. They complete nothing.

5.
A broken allure keeps history alive.
Seeing it wrecked, innocent, we forgive.

SATIESME

Aubain looked up. From where he sat in the lawn chair, he
could see two girls in orange kimonos waving. They
looked nice by the trees, their small hands waving prettily

against the green background. "They are quite exotic, the way
their little bodies move in the silk," he thought. "I should wave
to them." He did, and after a perfect giggle they

joined hands and ran off, looking back a few times as if
they wanted him to get up and come after them. Aubain
got up like a dancer in an old movie, glad to have

real girls in a real place to work to. For a man
like him, two girls in orange kimonos were the kind
of music that, in itself, is real, is a chance to mean

something as finished as a pretty girl whose mind
is given up to her twin so she can run. The chance
was a new mannerism, worked up out of the fine

reality that Aubain called music. With the girls
ahead of him, he ran as far as the place where clouds
met the lawn; from there, he saw the kimonos stop and dance

with each other in erotic figures, the four small hands
describing manners and curves in the green air. The lawn
moved. Aubain, caught up for the first time in clouds

and kimonos, moved as if he were in a ballroom with crown
medallions waltzing him to the stars. The two girls stopped
and came close. He heard their voices, but was just too far gone

to see anything but stars and the perfect twins that kept
on dancing somewhere. A little frightened, the two went home.
From where the clouds met the lawn, Aubain could feel something.
                                                                    Wrapped

up in his own two arms, he felt like the whole dream
that is the life of a mannerist. As prettily
as girls can, he danced a perfect curve in three-quarter time.

AESTHETE'S COMPLAINT

This world could never penetrate your mind
my dear. In short, the future isn't gay.
The verb "to be" is far too well defined.

What if tomorrow you should wake to find
your room a horror and your friends away?
This world could never penetrate your mind,

not even then. Suppose you looked behind
you, seeing no one, though you had heard me say
"the verb 'to be' is far too well defined"

as if my lips were at your ear? Combined
with thought, the words are real, yet I'm afraid
this world could never penetrate your mind

through chatter. Pictures then? No, be resigned
to terror. Life is better lost that way.
The verb "to be" is far too well defined

to tolerate much longer. Man's inclined
to dying; better dead than réchauffé.
This world could never penetrate your mind.
The verb "to be" is far too well defined.

NEAR RHINEBECK

When you arrive, the door is broken. Ironic,
isn't it, the note she left on the white
rug in the bedroom reading "I've crossed the river,
leaving you on the wrong side. Penelope."
The wrong side of what? The river. The old need
for hope you could not talk her out of. Panic

explains that kind of note, its queer tone, but panic
is here now, left behind with you. Ironic
as thieves in a fun house, there is your dumb need
of images to understand things: white
rug, white paper, red lines between blue, Penelope
in white coat walking across the frozen river.

Some years back there had been another river.
It ran down through tall bluffs to the city of panic.
At the green bridge it would heave and foam. "Penelope,
it is the live thread of both our lives. Ironic
lives wasted hawking images of white
clouds to whiter clouds," you'd say. She'd laugh. She would need

to more and more as your good years struck need
and took you north, away from the city. Upriver,
there was only the winding down to white
center and to the blind routine where panic
takes the name of a child or passion. Ironic
neighbors took to playing along. Penelope

hated it. Playing scenes from *Life with Penelope*
put the big scenes—Death, No Love—off. The need

you carried like side arms kept things ironic.
All marriage is staged irony, a river
dammed with garlands. In that country, panic
is what becomes of hope. She puts the white

coat on. When you arrive, the white
rug hands you the news. You've really won. Penelope
has gone and left you safe near Rhinebeck. Panic
behind her now, she crosses the ice from need
to the west bank. In that other country rivers
flow unchecked through tranquil cities. Ironic

clouds become white hopes. It is ironic
that panic is no different from need
in the end. Forget Penelope. Love the river.

III

OVER MANHATTAN

The dashboard's light was all the light. Outside,
the blue dividers, the dark towns that stay
where they are and make you miss them, thinned and flew.
Like nothing ever, the geography

of driving to New York through fog was a proof
for something. Seeing what you could not see,
this dark, that blue at the edges, you believed
the road, or possibly you felt a push

that left you secure because it lingered. All
that way, a local theism retrieved
good distance, fixed it up in the dark with towns,
dividers. In no light but the dashboard's, brief

locales became a part of New York. "You'd better
lie back," he said. "We won't be getting much sleep
with Drew there and his girlfriend yelling." You
saw headlights floating against the fog and thought

of windows on the East River: always them,
and always out of the same need to feel
like Dante, traveling through God. Asleep
then, with the prospect of harsh words and a cold

watch on the promenade before you, dreams
took over; the dark towns became complete
in other landscapes, other drives back home.
You went home through landscapes, other lives, another

long retrieve that ended up bad for all
of them, the girls included. You began
again, and for once, it was the place you really
saw that looked back. When an air horn woke you, part

of the last dream was still going. "You're alive,
then? There's a beer left I saved for you." With the fog
lifting, the damp ground held onto blue-
grey horizontals that moved as the car did. Thanks

to the warm beer most likely, that state of mind
where a good dream and the real place you had
it get along so well that a new one, made
out of both happens, took off from the view.

Over the sidewalk, in an oriel
window, one of those lamps you have always wanted
shone tiffany amber. From the chairs inside,
two figures looked down at you, and it made sense

that they bent into the light to laugh to each other
or to confess things. With the dark town in back,
all the light there was was the oriel's,
its part of New York compacted into two figures.

You whistled Satie's "Relâche" and they moved to it,
got up in costume, smiling as the car
went faster, as the windshield framed those first lights
across Jersey. Clear between the buildings, two girls

in costume tights were in love for sure, their blue
eyes stars over Manhattan. "Now what, chief?
The park or the highway?" Coming out by the art
museum, the last trees gave it up and you

knew why there were two of them, dark towns and blue
dividers for dreams, though how it had all made sense,
what with girls and the local gods behind
you, the East River back with its windows, only

a good wind or a cold watch in the dark
could tell you. No matter what, the blue-grey lines
and the warm beer had come down to something. Clear
between the buildings, there was a smile for stars,

blue eyes and towns for the city. "Drew's still up,
thank God. You go on while I park." It was the girlfriend's
yelling, the long, dark whistle down the hall
that brought you in and sat you down by the window.

JEROME AVENUE

Oblique now as before, there are these
insistent images: the sunlight
on brick walls, the tensed nude,
the sunlight on brick walls.

Kiss me quickly my Infanta, my White Face.

Even clouds are oblique now, the sky
as it runs backwards tears them.
In New York, I'd explain these. Here
I stare.

Kiss me quickly my Infanta, my White Face.

It is that part of life kept in images
we deny. The day says, "Look."
I can't. "How is it that you left her
naked, turned to that bright wall?"

I turn, and the sky turns east all over again.

RECALLING THE NAMES

The lights are Spanish, that is they change, they do
not chase the dark. In the livid dark of Southern
Boulevard, sudden cries and figures scare
you up the steps of a building. In the yellow
hall, you smell piss and hear three different radios.
That tells you everything, doesn't it? How twenty
years in the Bronx can teach you nothing but
a dumb routine, a set of pantomimes
in which you get scared or angry, wrecked or laid
depending on what it is you smell or hear
through the wall. If not, then tell about your day
with Anne at the Botanical Gardens, wind
making a pendant of the air above
your hillock. Where is it you go then to dodge
the maudlin story lines that always end
with Anne at the maudlin Gardens? The yellow hall.

    Where are the girls with the exotic names
    now? I woke up into a world where each
    disappeared into the hot rain settling
    through hot, still air like a green sweat or green cloud.

    I stayed with her on that street for one whole summer.
    We lay close to the floor and counted screams
    and flashes on the wall as they broke out.
    In her tight fist of a room, we sweated clouds.

What can you expect to become or love
next? After a while, the only thing to do
is to go back to what doesn't need you, to those

plain blocks where you can sit on the stoop and drink
until the ice cream man comes or until bed.
One summer, blimps flew overhead with electric
lights that spelled out "Save Water." Maybe this
year they'll return and you can have a reunion.
Maybe being unnecessary frees
a person the way it frees those blocks from having
to lead anywhere but to the Zoo or subway.
What begins now is the silence that won't
have anything to explain because it won't
be noticed. Go to the Gardens now. Walk into
the darkest building you can find and don't
say anything. Nobody will be surprised.

       Memory is the violence that calls
       things names and makes them return love for love,
       a clear look for a pathetic outcry. What
       can make a summer out of nothing but screams

       is screams. Call them "The Voices of Loveland." I
       do. What I know I remember settles through
       the air and hits the street like a green cloud.
       I remember the exotic names of girls.

Through heavy air, you look out over the Bronx
and count the streets you can see. Alone on a hot,
dark platform of the el you can see them swim.
Leaning against an ad for *Equus* through which bleed
two figures running along a white beach somewhere,
you look into the building across from you.
On a level with the top floor, you can see
into the one lighted window, into a white kitchen.
No one is visible. A pot on the stove boils.
A radio on the windowsill keeps playing.

When the train comes, you ride between cars for one
stop then get off. You hurry down and run
through the intermittent shadow under
the el. The streets smell of oranges and old
rain; they shout at you the whole way back
to that building. From the stairs, you can hear the radio.

NO MOMENT

The small bride is posed by the trees, and she escapes you.

For years, the grey trees have stood in the yard and blurred
like snapshots. Each spring, they blossom a little, white
florets blowing around on the grey branches
in twists, but no leaves come. The trees flourish. At night,

you can see them grabbing at the moon for its color.

It is hot for spring, and the color of the sky
has been lost. The bride is dressed now; her face appears
at a window, smiles and then frowns at the grey trees.
In the yard, the guests drink punch until someone steers

them to chairs near the white trellis. Here you lose track.

Look down. The white florets in the brown grass should tell
you something. As in a mirror that is all cluttered
with snapshots, they explain what the past means—the private
lives blown around through brief services and weathered

in twists. The days dress out in a bright pallor.

The special events, like florets, fall and then maunder
easily over unkept ground. It is how
they last in the changed place that is awful.
The bride frowns. The grey trees grab at the sky and now

the whole yard looks like a wild paraph that faded.

The occasion lasts, and there is always its one
dull pose, the familiar stand of shadows framing
the trellis. You need that; it is the flourish time
makes, its paraph and signal. In becoming

lost, you construed a part of it. The same day

begins with the morning star in the grey trees. West
of the yard, a big cloud blurs and looks threatening.
It is hot already as cicadas whirr
in the brown grass. She is awake now. Everything

hurries. Posed by the trees, she waves. For years,

you have flourished in a small life. The past has helped
you. Each spring, some florets have blown across the yard
to explain what time is, simply, and with a special
twist. Now she escapes you. Moved, the grey trees are blurred

in a signal manner. You grin. They almost sway.

ANIMAUX

Alone in an infected place,
one must admit the world seems small
enough. Superlatives enlarge
it some, but words remain abstract,
a world unto themselves, and so
are put aside in the sickroom, put
away that death might talk itself
to sleep.
      The night is no affair
of scenery, but rather one
of slide projectors, drink, and dull
resoundings in the other rooms.
The bulb burns through the photograph.
The drinks are emptied. The neighbors dream
of nothing or of Paradise,
and so are dead.
      The animal,
alone in an infected place,
begins to jabber. Worlds away
the human wakes—gregarious.

STEVENSON AND JAMES AT SKERRYVORE

They looked together at the Isle of Wight.
S. talked about how the boy in his new book
would go there looking for pirates and how he
would find them, singing, burying a box.

"He'll make the crossing in a boat he's made
by himself from packing crates. Louise, the girl
he pretends to hate but really likes, encourages
him. By the end, she'll have saved them both—twice."

The clear sky over the Isle of Wight was bluer
than the sickroom. In the mirror J. gave
S. for a joke because of a song they'd heard,
it made the walls look grey. "O tempt not

clemency," S. said, "to try his power.
He threats no deluge, yet foretells a shower."
It is by comparisons, by taking one
thing, putting it up next to another then

comparing that we make scenes and that the scenes
become sardanas. Klee next to a "Lucky Fisherman"
calendar. Dark Anne next to pale Mathilde.
Clear blue sky next to blue walls in a sickroom.

When S. recovered he went to the South Seas
and wrote about pirates who reform. He left
the mirror behind, figuring that sky
was sky. He was right and lived for years that way.

"The pirate helps Louise and the boy get back
to the little boat made out of packing crates.
As they paddle off, he waves and then goes back.
Louise and the boy remember him forever."

TOKENS

With none of the decor then, none
of the prettiness heart freaks for it-
self out of drab air, there is mind
caught scribbling: gaunt designs of what
fear changed or left to stand in white
rooms, as in amber, to cheat life.

It is, I'm certain, the same feeling.

There is also the collapse of life
into signs and tokens. You preserve
these, use the homeliest for comfort—
the woman's face inside a shell,
the white heart in amber. They turn fear
into the little designs you love.

It is, I'm certain, the same feeling.

MIGNONETTE

The metaphors are what has really happened. When
the stars go, it's a person going, or an old
religion folding like a lawn chair, only less
dramatic, less whatever you would call a girl
with cancer or a star that fell. The metaphors

are at the convent where she had so many friends,
so many things to talk about, and they are the blue
green of an ocean, only more like stars. The white
embroidery, her body white and smooth beneath
it, folded in a chair is wonderful to think

of when the moon's in Cancer. She would dream about
the lawn or of the convent moon where men betray
themselves. A lawn could only think of dreaming. Think
about a girl you saw by moonlight, dancing on
the lawn. You see a window seat from where you see

a chair in which a girl is dying. Cancer kills,
and only stars can help her. Mignonette, the love
of whom is dancing on the lawn like convent stars,
could never have religion, white as she could be
for anyone who talked to her or sat beside

her in the little chair, not even now with stars
about to fall and cancer. Metaphors are what
a girl depends on at a time like this, because
the way they work is musical, and music makes
you feel good, even if you're not religious. Life

is any convent, any constellation or
a chair to die in, dreaming of the way a lawn
can look. You looked at her again to see
a proof of something, but you didn't find it, didn't
betray yourself. The metaphors are what you said

would happen: stars around a chair, the cancer of
a girl who dances on the lawn and likes to talk
about religion when the moon's up. What you said
is that you dreamed of watching. Music dreamed. The silk,
what is so white around her folded body, watched.

GENEVIEVE DYING

You recapture elegance and fall back into
the pillow. On the wall you face there is
that drawing of St. John's head you copied and
had framed in Pavia. If you could see
what is now happening to you as he would,
through eyes refashioned by your own hand after
di Paolo, that elegance might last and see
you into the stillness only dying offers.

Closer to that stillness, you tilt your head
as though listening to a whisper pity
moves you to hear out and then acknowledge.
You face the tilted head of the saint, and as
the air around your bed becomes di Paolo's blue,
John's eyes, the eyes you worked a whole summer to
get right, are yours. You fall back into the flat,
still surface of the air you breathed in Pavia.

A FEW DISCRETIONS

1.
Afraid so much, and the real shock of a small
room webbed by things. It starts there, probably,
or as the book on a nightstand will, it offers
a system, making a clear line for once,
supporting the room by leading out of it,
nearer to something. By the window, then,
new modes are replacing old ones and the room,
still more than anything else visible,
responds as the light fails, as the one window
gives up entirely. With no outside,
winds lift the only alternatives to a webbed
room and those sounds, those smells from the bent trees
come in while the dark gets lively. There were parts
there. For months, the extreme lives had agreed
to each other. In the sad, old way, they are now
taking turns with winds, new roles supporting
the air in lamplight. The model works; the system
agrees to break down, as lives will, invisibly.

2.
He read aloud. The room, its clear line
outdistancing him, looked dull and cluttered.
Outside, a sunshower failed and green
blots smoked where the trees were, wisps of yellow
abstracting the heavy air into paint.
He turned his back on the view and read
a line about paladins. A thin
arm covered by a thin sleeve reached
for the book, its little hand suggesting

the kind of shadows that birds make crossing
a pond. He stuck a card in the book
and put it down next to the chipped vase
on the nightstand. More than anything,
he wanted to be alone in an empty
room in the dark, and happy. He
was with a friend in a bedroom. Sunlight
from the one window there was crowding
the walls with flares and depressions. Half
asleep, his friend pulled at the white strings
of her robe and hummed. He thought out loud.
"Each summer begins with a new poetry.
I read; I go to hotels with big
lawns and wait for my friend. For three months,
we stay in the room, afraid, no closer."

3.
The bent trees sputter in the sun,
Convinced of nothing.
In no real country,
The summer's abstract has begun

To hang on the bright air like chintz
On windows. The couple,
Asleep together
In the unfailing room, repeats

This dream—in open country, birds
Throw shadows over
A pool of water
And prophesy in major chords.

4.
It is almost scary how a few turns, a few
discretions in a familiar room can break
you. Only the line, the plumed flare twisting the moon-
light into shadows that work, that lead you out
to the bent trees on the lawn, can answer clearly.

My friend wakes up. Arranging the white strings
of her robe, she hums. Outside, the watery air
lifts in a faint breeze and suggests something
alien to both the room and summer:
a model, perhaps, or a quick sketch of a new

hotel in the snow country. When the breeze
drops, the room, convinced of its extreme
lives and unique distances, completes
an abstract, replacing the small view with pictures
of birds over a pond in open country.

Each summer comes down to a failed poetry.
A few discretions, lives from an old book
with pictures, continue to flare in the same room
and fall short of the window. In familiar starts,
the wind and lamplight respond as the dark gets lively.

HERE TO THERE

The biggest part of any story is rooms
and the things inside them. Everything else is too
vague, too uncertain in the way it happens,
changes or recites the lines it was
created to recite to live on its own.
I have a picture of an old friend naked,
her head tilted into shadow like
an Odalisque's. Whenever I look at it,
I remember first the room that it was taken
in, then her. I see the photograph
of a Brancusi head I'd tacked to the wall
behind her, then hers, tilted into shadow.
That lost room and the tacked-up photograph
keep her alive the way a mirror keeps
a ghost. Their strength is the reality
she uses. Seeing them, I see her live.

Supported by what surrounds it, an event,
even the brief kind, like some feelings (missing
a park or girl, nostalgia for the brickworks)
or a sudden chill, takes place as an
idea of those dumb things whose presence, by
supporting, sponsors it. Whatever happens
originates with them, leads back to them.
Not that my Odalisque was dreamed by the walls
exactly, or that missing her I act
out scenes from something that the desk or clock
radio ordered up. It's no occult
Cultural Geography that accounts
for how a life is channeled through its own days,

turned back upon itself for years sometimes,
for no reason, only to conclude as another
usual small tour of familiar rooms.

As in the theatre, where stage, props, scenery
pre-exist the action of a play
and outlast it and can bring it back, our rooms,
made into places by the events they've sponsored,
represent the mystery of how
things live and make us live. The origins
of change, they stand still, conduct what enters them.
My friend is what her picture lets her be.
What I remember is what the room, or rather
what that corner of it that I can see
keeps. Everything between us returns there
when it returns. Our story or anything
that happens happens as the interval
between one stillness and another. Rooms
fix an itinerary of still points
at the two ends of memory and join them.

A PERFECT SKYLINE

Betrayal that makes me dream makes me dream white.

It was the sky of the capital around
her I wanted. Nothing else I imagined,
neither the perfect skyline nor the words
I had her say, was at all necessary.

"I am yours as all things here are yours, for nothing."

That sky is the set of her best scene. It keeps
the secret of how she came to be here and why
I wanted her at all with half a world
collapsing inside me. I think of her, see her.

Betrayal that makes me dream makes me dream white.

THERIOT COVE

It is the lights of the boathouse that lead you. Back
in your own good place, the fear, the opposed estrangements
flare in the blue bulbs and are over for good.
The plash of water against the boats sounds good
to you, and the boathouse bar is the only place
on the island where you can drink and hear it. You
drink gimlets and look out over the indigo
backwater, thinking that each blue flash is yours
and that the boats are a symbol for a kind of intense
experience—each boat, blue and then black as back-
water, imaging part of it. The fear
was the part you ran from; the estrangements had carried
you as far as this. Think back. Having lived with no
one for a long time, you started thinking about
a trip to the island. You remembered how safe
it was and how much fun you had always had
in the months you lived there, the summer people crowding
your time with boathouse parties. The lights on the pier
would announce those parties: blue for formal, light green
for swimsuits, and red for come-as-you-are. Light green
was your favorite and still, it was that that caught
you short, that made you remember just how far
you had come and why and how afraid of it all
becoming final you really were. What the fear
led back to was a brief interval, les nuits vertes,
in which you surpassed the island and reached a life's
work, suddenly. After that interval, estrangements,
the appalled white nights between then and the remembrance.

And so you came around and remembered, smiling

like a child in a downtown store when it finds
a mirror. Driving back, you could see the towns
disappearing, could imagine the boathouse green
against stars and everything mirrored to a blur
in backwater. For the last few miles, summer lightning
flashed over the water in a regular panic.
It kept on flashing. When you stopped, the blue lights
that meant formal flared against a blank sky and led
you in, overruling everything. Without fear
and without estrangements to regret, you can drink
your drink now, and watch as the formal couples dance
to the plash of water against boats. It is your own
good place and the only place on the island where
a symbol matters, where colors mean and prescribe.

HOMAGE

I have looked into the air between my hands
and seen the white ovals, the abstracted, green
or blue eyes of maps of cities. Every face

accuses: the wrong of exile, the worse wrong
of pity, which is like the rain on metal
railings or like the sounds at night that fix

themselves to the shadows of small leaves and change
as the wind changes. I even name them sometimes.
Ellen. Madrid. The one whose eyes were too

close to one another, who was called Berthe.
The naming puts them at a distance and down
to where a thing can be fought for, lost, and then

forgotten easily. In the abandoned,
white cities of a republic, the names are eyes
on walls. The rain, if it rains, makes them luminous.

I have looked into the faces between my hands
and seen years fail. The abandoned cities reclaim
themselves for themselves and shine with exile, with pity.